SEESAW

LOVE LIFE FRIENDSHIP

DR. RAVINDRAPAL SINGH
MUZALDA (KAVIRP)

Contents

Hard Work

Hard Work, Hard work,

Do the hard work.

First of all set your AIM,

Don't see back ward from the GAME.

Do the hard work for the DAY'S AND NIGHT,

Think Positive and do always RIGHT.

Don't think for the Great FRUIT,

Keep stand the trees on the Root.

When you go for the final,

You are ready for doing the things ACTUAL.

If you are very nervous,

Show to all of them that you are TREMENDOUS.

In Exam Keep work hands in PACE,

Because slow and steady wins the RACE.

Tell the success to you to CALL,

You are the person who can defeat ALL.

At point where destiny & Success MEET,

The taste of success is so Sweet.

Happiness all around your Soul,

As you are Very near to the GOAL.

This is the result of your HARD WORK

Do the HARD WORK & HARD WORK.

If u are disappointed Never you CRY,

Do the hard work, again you TRY.

One day the success will knock your door,

Do the hard work success will always be more.

Friendship - A GOLD MEDAL IN A RACE OF LIFE

Away from the family

Finding for a friend truly,

I try to know them, they try to know me

Friend for a life time, I am trying to see.

Without friends life is unimportant,

Like the gravity of the earth is constant,

We are really missing them now,

Without them no today & no now.

Something between us makes close ship

And I think this is only our friendship.

Memories are with me when I'm apart from them

A true friend is in my life I claimed.

Remembering them as heart without sound

I can feel them in the worldly Crowd

Trust is the Ocean, Friends are like a ship

This is my idea of a True friendship...!

क्या पहचान मेरी...

कल कोई पहचान नहीं होगी मेरी

बूंद हूं मे आज बारशि की

आंसू बन जाऊं पलको का तेरी

जब भी तूने कोई ख्वाहशि की

कल कोई पहचान नहीं होगी मेरी

जब शाख से टूट जाऊंगा मैं

रख लेना मुझे तुम याद बनाकर

जब फिर उड़ता फिरूं सूनी इन राहों में

कल कोई पहचान नहीं होगी मेरी

ढल जाऊंगा बनकर मैं सूरज

ख्याल ना आए कभी अकेला हूं मैं

आवाज देना मुझे जब भी हो जरूरत

कल कोई पहचान नहीं होगी मेरी

पंछी बन उड़ जाऊंगा लेकर सारी यादें

ना सोचना भूल जाएगा वो तुम्हें

उसे भी याद है तुझ से जुड़ी हर बातें

कल कोई पहचान नहीं होगी मेरी

मांगे तू कुछ और टूट जाऊंगा बनके मैं तारा

कर नहीं सकता रोशन दुनिया को मगर

कर जाऊंगा रोशन मैं जग तेरा सारा

<u>ऐ खुशी...</u>

गमो से है क्या लेना हमें

खुशी ही है ज़िन्दगी का रास्ता

एक पल कभी हुई नम भी आंखें

तो भूलकर गम को, खुशी से है आगे बढ़ना

बेपरवाह गमों से दूर हम चलते चले

इन राहों में खुशियों की तलाश कर रहे

कभी यादों में ढूंढ़ कर कभी कल में

इस बात से है अंजान के खुशी है खुद में

अनचाहो गमो को मिटा कर रेतों से
खुशी की लहरों से हम आगे हैं बढ़ रहे
फकिरों और गमो को उड़ा कर आसमानों में
ऐ जिंदगी, बता दे की हम हैं ख़ुशी से जी रहे...

मेरी ख़्वाहिशियें...

भीड़ भरी इस दुनिया में
ढूँढू उसे जिसे मैंने है खोया
तेरी कीमत तो नहीं जनता था पर
हीरे से भी ज़्यदा तुझे मैंने है पाया
मिला एक जो यार मुझे
रहने न दे कभी तन्हा
तेरा साथ पाकर बन गया हूँ
अपने ही प्यार का गवाह
मकसद मिला यूँ जीने का
ज़िन्दगी में मुझे ऐसे
कर दिया तेरे प्यार के सूरज ने
ज़िन्दगी में उजाला जैसे
जब तुम हो गम में, या हो खुश
बाटना हर पल साथ मेरे
चाँद होता है रात के संग जैसे
मैं भी रहूँगा वैसे ही साथ तेरे
तुम साथ रहना, कांटों से भरी राह तक

मुझे साथ तेरे मंज़िल पर है जाना
अब मिल गया है साथ तेरा तो
सखि लिया है काँटों ने भी महकना
तू चलना साथ मेरी मंज़िलों के रास्ते
कोसो दूर होगी तुझसे तेरी तन्हाई
मुड़ कर न देखना पीछे न मिलूँगा मैं
क्यूंकि बिन गया हूँ मे तेरी ही परछाई

<u>तेरी खुशियां...</u>

अकेला नहीं मैं, तेरा एहसास है साथ
नीला आसमां यूं ही नहीं बनके साया साथ हो
खुशियां तुझे इतनी मिले
गम का कहीं निशान ना हो
हो कभी खुशी, कभी गम
जिंदगी का यही दस्तूर है
चाहूं बस खुशी मैं तेरी
छाया यह दोस्ती का सुरूर है
गम आए कभी जिंदगी में तेरे
तो काँटो को अलग कर दूंगा
तेरी खुशी मेरी खुशी बन जाएगी
जब भी तू मेरे साथ होगा
इंद्रधनुष के सात रंगो से
जिंदगी में तेरी बिखेर दूं
फूलो की खुशबू, चांद की चांदनी
नहीं जानती, मेरे लिए क्या है तू
कोई ख्वाहिश करके तो देख

खुशी के लिए कुछ भी कर जाएंगे
दुखी कभी देखूं इतनी हिम्मत मुझ में नहीं
खुश रहे यही दुआ रब से करेंगे

<u>कैसे कहूँ...</u>

चाहने लगा में तुझे क्यों
पहले तो न किसी को इतना चाहा
इस चाहत को तुझे में कैसे कहूँ...
इतनी परवाह तेरी है मुझे क्यों
ना की परवाह किसी की भी इतनी कभी
इस परवाह को तुझे में कैसे कहूँ...
तम्मन्ना है खुश रख हमेशा तुझे
न पहले की कोई ऐसी तम्मन्ना
इन तमन्नाओ को तुझे में कैसे कहूँ...
हो गई कैसी ये दिल्लगी तुझसे क्यों
पहले तो न हुआ ऐसा कभी
इस दिल्लगी को यारा में कैसे कहूँ...
तुझे न याद कर तो बेकरार हो जाता हूँ
ये बेकरारी तो पहले न थी कभी
इस बेकरारी को जाना कैसे कहूँ...
चाहता हूँ कैसे बया करूँ मेरे जज़्बात दिल के
नए से है ये जज़्बात, जो न थे पहले कभी
इन जज़्बातों को यारा में कसे कहूँ...

<u>I feel you...</u>

When the wind touches me as always
Like you are touching me
But I feel you...
When the sun's heat makes me burn
Like you sometimes angry upon me
But I feel you...
When someone hugs their loved ones
Like that the rivers are meeting the oceans
But I feel you...
When you need me I was there always
Like that the need of night for the day
But I need you…
When the rain kisses the soul of my heart
Like that you kissed me last
But I feel you…
When the faded memories of mine are with you
May be after sometimes you will forget
But then also I will feel you...

<u>प्यार...</u>

पढ़ो तो एक शब्द
न मानो तो कुछ भी नहीं
मानो तो एक एहसास
न मानो तो है ही नहीं
प्यार है एक गहरा समंदर
तू ही तू बसा है मेरे अंदर
आईना में जो देख खुद का

अक्स दिखाई देता है तेरा

प्यार कब हुआ और हवाओं की तरह बहता चला गया

वो भी इससे और मैं भी इस लहर से बेखबर हो गया

प्यार का रंग मुझ पर जो चढ़ गया

के कोई और रंग न तेरे सिवा भाया

एक हो उदास तो दूजे को नींद कहाँ आती है,

कहने को अलग है लेकिन तुझमें मेरी जान बसती है

तुम क्या हो मेरे लिए,

यह समझना मुमकिन नहीं मेरे लिए

ये समझ लो मुझे साँसों की नहीं,

ज़रूरत है तुम्हारी जीने के लिए

प्यार एक प्यारा सा एहसास है,

मेरी हर एक साँस में तुझे जीना चाहता हूँ

तभी तो ये रिश्ता दुनिया में ख़ास है,

हर एक धड़कन में धड़कना चाहता हूँ

<u>You are...</u>

You are the thought that start each morning,

The conclusion of each day.

You are the stars that I need every night,

And disappears in the beginning of the day.

You are the seashore of my life,

That my every wave will comes to meet you.

You are the rain of my wishes which I m waiting for,

That will drench upon my thirsty heart's land.

You are my one of the favourite songs,

Which I want to listen again and again.

You are the flower that blooms in my heart,
This spread its fragrance everywhere.
You bring the smile on my face,
Reason behind is only you are...

मुझे तू दे दे...

गम की हो धूप मुझ पर
खुशी कि तू छाऊं दे दे
गहरे हो कभी दर्द मेरे
दोस्ती का तू मरहम दे दे
राहों में काटें ही मिले हैं
फूल कभी तू बिछा दे
हमेशा साहिल खाली मेरे रहे
बनकर लहर तू छू ले
रह न जाऊं तन्हा में
याद तेरी तू मुझे दे दे
कैसे कटेंगे पल यह मेरे
एक लम्हा तेरा तू मुझे दे दे
तन्हा हो गया हूं मैं
यार महफिल तू मुझे दे दे
लडख़डा ना जाए कदम मेरे
साथ तेरा तो मुझे दे दे

फिर तेरी...

होगा जो जिंदगी में अंधियारा कभी
फिर तेरी वो रोशनी बन जाऊं

ना हो संग तेरे साथ किसी का
फिर तेरा वो साथ बन जाऊं
गम की रात छाई हो कभी जो तुझ पर
खुशियों से भरा वह दिन बन जाऊं
अकेले से तन्हा हो जाओ जब कभी
फिर तेरी वो महफिल बन जाऊं
जो तू मांगे खुदा से
तेरी वो इबादत बन जाऊं
कदम जो कभी तो रखे धूप में
फिर तेरी वो छांव बन जाऊं
कांटे जो कभी चुभे तुझे इन राहों में
उन राहों का वो फूल बन जाऊं
कोई ख्वाहिश करे तू तारों से
और टूटता हुआ वो तारा बन जाऊं
साया हो साथ तेरा हमेशा
सोच के तेरा वो आसमां बन जाऊं
तू जो जिंदगी से करे आरजू
फिर तेरी वो जिंदगी बन जाऊं

<u>What you are for me...?</u>

You are my morning light
You are my dark night
When you are with me
You kept my a world beside
You are my shadow
You make me laugh the way u can do
You are my world

How important you are to me never you know

You are my life's paradise

Will tell the world with a heavy voice

Footsteps of you and me are on the seashore

Waves of happiness will be more and more

You are the results of my prayers

I was sought you from the god

I see you in my life's mirror

As you are presents in my thoughts

You can be hiding with me

But never can me

Flowers fragrance is with me

But pain is inside me

You make me smile, laugh

The person is you are

You promise me, I will be with you

And how far you are

Memories of rainbow

Can never be go

How much ILOVE YOU

Never will I show

<u>Remember One Thing...</u>

There is someone who will be with you,

Don't look backwards as I had become your shadow.

There is someone who will walk with you,

No matter how thorny the way is.

There is someone who can't live without you,

No matter how I m important to you.

There is someone who is waiting for the spring,

No matter I m the leaves of the last summer.

There is someone who will be shatter for you,

No matter if you only will broke me into pieces.

There is somebody who can wait for you,

No matter how long the life is.

Never forget me from your heart and memories,

There is someone who is living just for you....

<u>The night knows</u>

Those loneliness I m living in you,

You might be not aware of it,

But the night knows.

Those tears which belongs to you,

Oceans of tears you never know,

But the night knows.

The shadow which disappears in that night,

You will not even feel that,

But the night feels.

You have seen me smiling but not my pain behind,

If you had walked there I have shattered into pieces,

But the night knows.

You told me you will always with me,

But only the moon and stars are with me,

But the night knows.

<u>Heals Me...</u>

When I was gone through unbearable pain
It was the time which heals me
When the old scar got wounded again
It was your feathery touch which heals me
When there was darkness surrounding me
It was the silver lining of light which heals me
When my shadow is not even with me
It was the another shadow which heals me
When buried deep in the soil, others don't know I was a seed
It was the rain which heals me
When others didn't understand my love, my feelings, and my pain
It was you and at least you can feel me
When it was my tears has got dried in eyes
But it was the night which heals me
When holding your hand, graceful long journey with you
It was the Destination which heals me
When I have an ocean of emotions inside me
It was the pen and paper which heals me

<u>ऐ ज़िंदगी...</u>

ठोकरें गर जो लगीं मुझे
तू ही रास्तों का पत्थर, तू ही सहारा
तू अगर साथ है मेरे
न ही मैं कभी ठहरा, ना ही हारा

ऐ ज़िंदगी...
ना साथ छोड़ना कभी मेरा
न कड़कती धूप में, न ठंडी छाओं में
आग़ोश में तू मुझे भर लेना
मैं भी भर लूंगा तुझे मेरी इन बाँहों में
ऐ ज़िंदगी...
तू साथ छोड़ना ना मेरा
न किसी किनारे से, न कोई साहिल से
तू ही है तो होगा साथ मेरा
हर राह पर, मेरी हर मंज़िल पे
ऐ ज़िंदगी...
ना दूर जाना मुझसे
चाहे हसीं हो या हो आँसू हम से
मुझे प्यार है तुझसे
तेरी हर खुशी से, तेरे हर ग़म से
ऐ ज़िंदगी...

ज़िंदगी और क्या है

तुझको जवाबों में ढूंढ कर
मेरे हर सवालों को आसान कर
फिर भी क्यों लग रही है उलझन
ज़िंदगी और सवाल क्या है.
तुझको ख़्वाबों में पीरो कर
मेरे हौंसलों को बढ़ा कर
टूटू सा गया हूँ मैं जाने क्यों
ज़िंदगी और ख्याल क्या है

गनि गनि कर दी हैं जो खुशियां
करके ये गमो की मुझ पर बारिश
बेहिसाब हैं मेरे गमो का पुलिंदा
ज़िन्दगी तेरे और हिसाब क्या हैं
कुछ तेरा न कहना, कुछ मेरा न सुनना
लफ़्ज़ खामोश न रह जाए कभी
कुछ तो ऐ ज़िन्दगी मुझे भी बताना
ज़िन्दगी और बात क्या हैं

<u>भावना की ए जिंदगी...</u>

ए जिंदगी, मेरी प्यारी जिंदगी
खूबसूरत दुनिया से न्यारी जिंदगी
आज तूने बहुत कुछ दिया हैं मुझे
कल जो छीना था उससे ज़्यादा दिया हैं मुझे
जो आंसू थे उनसे भी हंसी दी मुझे
कल जो मजिलें थी आज उन पर चलना सिखाती हैं
ए जिंदगी...
कभी कडवी तो कभी मीठी हैं जिंदगी
कभी आंधी तो कभी दिए की लौ हैं जिंदगी
कभी मेरी तो कभी किसी और की हैं जिंदगी
कभी बुरी तो कभी सबसे प्यारी हैं जिंदगी
ए जिंदगी
पत्तियों की तरह लहराती हैं जिंदगी
कभी नदी में बहती हैं जिंदगी
अरमानों की तरह भी बह जाती हैं तू
तो कभी पंछियों की तरह चहचहाती हैं जिंदगी

ऐ ज़िंदगी...

<u>Whenever The Life...</u>

Whenever, I have been in the dark.
The life showed me the rays of light.
Whenever, I have walked on the thorns in my way.
The life has showered with the flowers on it.
Whenever, my dreams shattered in pieces.
The life has given me courage to fulfil.
Whenever, I have no plans to execute.
The life has another for me.
Whenever, I was alone in this world.
The life was with me in the form of air.
Whenever, I have no shelters over me.
The life has a sky for me.
Whenever, the people laugh at my failures.
The life gave me the second chance to success.
Whenever, there's nobody to support me.
It was the life who always.

<u>सफ़र यह ज़िंदगी का...</u>

ख़्वाबों का यूँ टूट जाना
टूट कर काँच सा बिखिर जाना
फिर उन्ही ख़्वाबों को संजोना
सफ़र यह ख़्वाबों का....
ख्वाहिशयें हैं मेरी हज़ार

उनका य॒ु कभी रह जाना अधूरा

देखना फिर भी न भूली मेरी नज़र

सफर यह ख़्वाहिशों का...

मंज़िल का था लंबा इंतज़ार

देखना मुड़ कर न था गवारा

करता रहा कोशिशों में हर बार

सफर यह हौसलों का...

जाए जहाँ तक नजर रास्तें ही थे

खुले नीले आसमानों के नीचे

ज़मीन को तय मुझे ही करना था

सफर यह ज़िंदगी का...

ज़िन्दगी – एक उमीद है

बहुत कुछ छीना जो मुझसे

उससे ज़्यदा कि उमीद है तुझसे

कभी जो आँसू दिये है गर

देंगी तू ही हसीं भी मुझे

कड़वे एहसास जो भी करा दिए

तो मिसरी सी मीठी भी है ज़िन्दगी

तूफ़ान आंधियों तुने जो भी दिए

ठंडी हवा सी भी है ज़िन्दगी

सूखे पत्तों सी अगर भखिरी है

तो लहराती वादियों सी भी है ज़िन्दगी

कल कल बहती नदिया जैसी है

तो गहरे समंदर सी भी है ज़िन्दगी

गर मैं गिरि भी जाऊ ठोकर खाकर

तो फरि उठ खड़ा करना ज़िन्दगी

अरमानो ं से अगर बैठा मैं हार कर

तो आसमानो ं से ऊँचे हौंसले करना ज़िन्दगी

<u>रूप की ऐ ज़िन्दगी...</u>

जीते रहने की सजा दे ज़िन्दगी ऐ ज़िन्दगी

अब तो मरने की सजा दे ज़िन्दगी ऐ ज़िन्दगी

मैं तो अब ऊब गया हूँ क्या यही है कायनात

बस यह आइना हटा दे जिंदगी ऐ ज़िन्दगी

ये मुझे एहसास हैं की इस कैद से कर दे रिहा

वर्ना दीवाना बना दे ज़िन्दगी ऐ ज़िन्दगी

ढूंढने निकिला था तुझको और खुद को खो दिया

तू ही अब मेरा पता दे ज़िन्दगी ऐ ज़िन्दगी

बेरंग कोरे से पन्नो ं पर स्याही डाल कर

तस्वीरें प्यारी सी तू बना दे जिंदगी ए जिंदगी

हौसलो ं को तो तोड़ भी दे अगर

मेरी आंखें नही ं भूल देखना ख्वाब ए जिंदगी

<u>**"Dream which Motivates Me"**</u>

Dream, when you hear this word, what first comes in your mind. The dream which we see with closed eyes in the night. When I will tell you to describe your dream you will think and start explaining the fantasy you saw in your dream. Dream is not same for everyone, not for you, not for me it will be different for different people. Everybody has its very own dream that everyone lives for, it's something that everybody experience once in a life time.

Everybody has a dream and everybody has different dream, and at every stage of life, every way of life, everybody has a different dream to fulfil.

A child, who has a dream just saw with a closed eyes & somebody has a beautiful dreams to be remember and somebody has a fear of dream to come and some body has escaping from the puzzle of their dream and somebody has run away from their dream. For the child, they have dream to become something from the very beginning of their life, when they can able to interpret what the dream is.

For the young they have something to live their future in their dreams. All the peoples have different perspective of their dream. They know actually a dream is, what to dream, what to do for a dream, what a dream has a consequences of it, what dream has a power to change your life's is future.

For me, dream is not just a word. It is something to live for, something to breath, something to see with open eyes, something that never let you sleep to achieve, something I can walk for a million miles, something I smell fragrance of flowers in every breath. My dream is everything that I can't live without, can't breathe without, and can't hear my heart beats without. It's something is drains in my veins.

For me, when I was nothing, I feel that, I was just a thorn of my own life. Who just comes to give pain to others? When I was felt alone, nobody to enthusiasm me, to encourage me. Nobody was close to me for support. For me to achieve my dreams, have spend my sleepless nights, without movies, without my best friends for a long time, deactivate my facebook account, switch off my mobile for a long time, months without shaved my beard. In my sleepless nights my partner in crime is my tea and my slow songs which give positiveness in my blood to achieve my dream. From my school days to graduation and then to my post graduation I have dream to become and successful doctor. In between those days, the day comes when I was shattered how many times, the ups and downs of the my shattered dream, which only knows by me. The journey on which I had walked alone is not so easy till my destination come.

My father and mother, brother and best friends, who always supports me, always encourages me, never let me down when I need them, they also dreaming that he could make their dream come true of becoming a doctor one day. And today, my dream has come true and become a MD doctor. And today when I looking back at my past struggle my foot prints are still there. Someone once said beautifully "If you have to walk million miles, than just start walking your 1st step" and then just sees how beautifully the journey will come true and you will remember the journey at last.

For me, my dream is my identity by which all will know me as today. This is the dream which I saw with open eyes and today achieved at a priceless cost. This is the idea of my dream. This is my dream which motivates me to do so to achieve my dream.

About Book

If you have imagined a "SEESAW", there are two sides: Love & Friendship which is balanced in between by the Life. This magazine will take you to the roller coaster ride and ups and downs in various phase of life. Not everybody is facing such phases, but at some point of time they will or gone through it. I hope you will like it this poetry book and it make sense to understand you and realise how the Life is in between love and friendship. And last not but the least, Thank you so much "Conscience Works Publication" who took my work, my poetry and publishing in the form of this beautiful book and giving me a platform to achieve my dream to come true.

My Bio

"Those loneliness I m living in you,

You might be not aware of it,

But the night knows..."

He is Dr. Ravindrapal Singh Muzalda (KaviRp). He has done MBBS, MD (RadioDiagnosis). Apart from his study. As he told that he is not a perfect Poet from the very beginning or has any knowledge of poem writing. But then one day he took a pen and start writing his thought and feelings stuck in mind that he want to write it down. This gave a birth of his inner child of poetry within him. He is now a budding quote writer and a poet. And he loves to write on Love, Life, Nature, Heart break and various other genre and themes. And now it's one of his favourite hobbies and loves to do so in his free time. His others hobbies includes drawing, loves to listening songs, cooking, gardening. He is also worked as a Co-Author for many anthologies. He published almost more than 10 published poems in various platforms. This is his first solo anthology as a Writer and it is so special to him and had a special place in his heart. You can Shower your love and support to him by get connected on Instagram - @kavirp08 and Your Quote app @kavirp. And last but not the least he Thanks to the compiler for this anthology and gave chance to explore his unfolded wings of thoughts.